THE WAR
WORKS HARD

الحرب تعمل بجد

DUNYA MIKHAIL

THE WAR WORKS HARD

الحرب تعمل بجد

TRANSLATED BY ELIZABETH WINSLOW

INTRODUCTION BY SAADI SIMAWE

A NEW DIRECTIONS BOOK

Some of these poems were first published in *Poetry International*, *Mizna*, *Modern Poetry in Translation*, *Circumference*, *Words Without Borders*, and *World Literature Today*.

Book design by Sylvia Frezzolini Severance
Manufactured in the United States of America
New Directions Books are printed on acid-free paper.
First published as New Directions Paperbook 1006 in 2005
Published simultaneously in Canada by Penguin Books Canada Limited

Library of Congress Cataloging-in-Publication Data

Mikhail, Dunya, 1965–
  [Al-Harb Ta'mal Bijid. English]
  The war works hard / Dunya Mikhail ; translated by Elizabeth Winslow,
  introduction by Saadi Simawe.
    p. cm.
  ISBN 0-8112-1621-7 (alk. paper)
  I. Winslow, Elizabeth, 1976– II. Mikhail, Dunya, 1965– Al-Harb
  Ta'mal Bijid. English. Selections. III. Title.
  PJ7846.I392H3713 2005
  892.7'36—dc22

                          2004028184

New Directions Books are published for James Laughlin
by New Directions Publishing Corporation
80 Eighth Avenue, New York, NY 10011

CONTENTS

Introduction by Saadi Simawe   *vii*

ONE. THE WAR WORKS HARD (2004)

Bag of Bones   3

Shoemaker   5

The War Works Hard   6

The Game   8

The Prisoner   9

A Drop of Water   10

Inanna   11

An Urgent Call   13

Non-Military Statements   15

Between Two Wars   17

Tough Rose   19

The Jewel   20

A Voice   21

Travel Agency   22

O   23

Santa Claus   24

Buzz   25

Crashed Acts   26

Snowstorm   27

To Any Other Place   29

I Was In A Hurry   31

America   33

Silent Movie   40

Laheeb and the City   41

The Rocking Chair   42

Traces   43

The Foreigner   44

Five Minutes   46

TWO. FROM **ALMOST MUSIC** (1997)

The Cup   51

The Resonance   53

The Artist Child   54

The Departure of Friends   56

A Tombstone   57

The Theory of Absence   58

Nothing Here is Enough   59

What's New?   60

The Pomegranate Seeds   61

With One Look From Him   62

An Orange   63

THREE. FROM **THE PSALMS OF ABSENCE** (1993)

Behind the Glass   67

The Nun   69

The New Year   70

Transformations of the Child and the Moon   71

The Chaldean's Ruins   72

The Shadow of a Tear   74

Pronouns   75

Notes   77

INTRODUCTION
DUNYA MIKHAIL: A POETIC VISION OUT OF THE IRAQI ASHES

first became aware of Dunya Mikhail in Miriam Cooke's 1996 volume titled *Women and the War Story,* which is a study of Arab women writers' response to war in Algeria, Palestine, Lebanon, and Iraq. In her discussion of Mikhail's *Diary of a Wave Outside the Sea* (1995), Cooke discerned and analyzed the book's double condemnation of the two warring sides as equally detrimental to the humanity of their people and the humanity of their enemy. *Diary of a Wave Outside the Sea* was published in Baghdad while the author was still living there, but the Iraqi fascist authorities were not initially able to identify its anti-war spirit. However, in the next few months, Mikhail would become terrified by increasingly systematic harassment from the regime until eventually, like most Iraqi writers, she could no longer keep her promise to stay in her country and thus fled first to Jordan and then to the United States.

Dunya Mikhail speaks and writes in three languages. A member of the Iraqi Christian minority, her native languages are both Aramaic (the ancient language of the pre-Islamic indigenous Iraqi Christians) and Arabic. English is her third language, which she learned in Iraqi high school, and college. Once in the U.S., Mikhail pursued her higher education and earned in 2001 an M.A. in Arabic from the Department of Near Eastern Studies, Wayne State University. Upon completion of her graduate work, she has been devoted to what she enjoys most: teaching Arabic.

Mikhail has impressively renovated the genre of the war poem in modern Arabic poetry by boldly introducing new techniques with a new vision. Instead of employing slogans and dead metaphors and political clichés that have blunted much of modern Arabic poetry, Mikhail writes about devastating successive wars within and against her country with a childlike intimacy and vulnerable sensibility. Her imagination is so immense that it embraces and synthesizes layers of literary traditions from ancient Mesopotamian mythology, to Biblical and Qur'anic poetics, to the latest techniques of Western modernism.

Since the mid-1980s, Mikhail has published five volumes of poetry. In all five volumes, war and fascism are crucial themes that inform her poetic vision. The subversive, clear-eyed speaker persistently unmasks the official glorification of war by trenchantly highlighting the shattered humanity among the rubble and the ruins. I read these volumes with such an intense mixture of pleasure and pain that I wanted to have some of the poems translated into English for an anthology of modern Iraqi poetry I was editing, *Iraqi Poetry Today*. Mikhail's poetic celebration of the human versus the debilitating ideological earned her the prestigious Human Rights Watch Award for Freedom of Writing in 2001.

The most striking aspect of Dunya Mikhail's poetry is its unique ability to surprise the reader's imagination and sensibility. An exhilarating ability to restore our pristine awe in our encounter with the things in the universe lies, it seems to me, in Mikhail's magical, childlike vision of the world, including her innovative rendition of the Arabic language. She plays with words as a child plays with countless colored toys that assume a fantastic life of their own in the child's imagination. That magical life of words, liberated from their prosaic connotations, sends shocks of guilt for what humans in war and oppression have done to each other, and pleasure and poignancy for the beauty of the universe. In most of the poems in this volume, the speaker seems as vulnerable and as subversive as the child in the famous tale of "The Emperor's New Clothes," who shames us into remembering our lost innocence and courage.

The poems in *The War Works Hard* were written, though not necessarily published, between 1985 and 2004, the darkest years in the history of Iraq and the period that witnessed the climax of American intervention that began in 1963 when the Baath party was brought to power by a U.S.-backed military coup. Saddam was a young officer at the time. Thus to many Iraqis, the American war against Iraq actually started on February 8, 1963 when the Baath junta, aided by U.S. intelligence from Kuwait, took over Baghdad. During the first two days of battle, more than 30,000 Iraqis who fiercely resisted the fascist coup were massacred. Traditional Iraqi prisons ran out of space, and schools, nurseries, and stadiums were turned into prisons and chambers for the most sophisticated torture methods with tools imported from the West.

Born in 1965, at the juncture of the most atrocious campaign the Baath party waged to trounce the smallest pockets of popular resistance, Dunya Mikhail's imagination was saturated with horror stories of imprisonment, torture, death, disappearances, massacres, and rape; she was surrounded by uprootedness and endless wars. Although it is almost impossible to historicize pain and fear because they tend to overawe consciousness as cosmic and metaphysical, chronologically speaking, the poetry in this volume is divided into three overlapping periods: a) the most recent poems, the ones written after the fall of Saddam Hussein such as "Bag of Bones," "Inanna," and "An Urgent Call" b) poems written after the poet's migration to the U.S. in 1996, such as "America," "Snowstorm," "Shoemaker," "The Jewel," "A Voice," "Travel Agency," "Buzz," "Crashed Acts," "I was in a Hurry," "The Rocking Chair," "Traces," "The Foreigner," and "Five Minutes" c) poems written in Baghdad during the Iraq-Iran war (1980-1988), the Gulf war of 1991, and the genocidal sanctions. Among these are "Between Two Wars," "Santa Claus," "To Any Other Place," and all the poems selected from *Almost Music* (1997) and *Psalms of Absence* (1993). It is significant that the volume opens with "Bag of Bones," a poem about the dead in a mass grave, those just "liberated" after the fall of the dictator, who never cared to give "death certificates." The poem, while lamenting the erasure-to-the-bone of identities, attempts, through Iraqi mothers and lovers searching for their loved ones, to restore, by sheer power of love, a sense of humanity to the bones and skulls.

Evidently, Mikhail's vision, innovative in the Arabic literary tradition, requires fresh poetics. Thus, in her poems, the Arabic language is liberated from traditional clichés of idiom and of style; and the classical metrical patterns, which have long fallen into monotony, are re-tuned into new intimate rhythms. Dead metaphors are resurrected and transformed into delicate, intimate, colorful verbal butterflies. For any reader familiar with the Arabic poetic tradition and sensibility, Mikhail's poems are refreshing and uplifting. Her vision, for instance, in the title poem, "The War Works Hard," is unparalleled in its quiet and therefore more effective subversion of war ideologies, in which the staunchest warmonger usually hides behind the thickest rhetoric of peace and humanity. In a poetic tradition that views the author as the absolute source of meaning, the whispering irony and the vulnerability of the speaker in this poem constitute an inspiring break from the monomaniacal tyranny—a break that opens space for the readers to share in pondering these uncanny images:

> The war continues working, day and night.
> It inspires tyrants
> to deliver long speeches,
> awards medals to the generals
> and themes to poets.
> It contributes to the industry

of artificial limbs,
provides food for flies,
adds pages to the history books,
achieves equality
between killer and killed

The key to the power of the poem is its speaker's ironic stance
and the childlike matter-of-fact images. Although this poem was
written in Baghdad, with the Iraq-Iran war and 1991 Gulf war
in mind, the poet was not able to publish it in Arabic until she
left Iraq.

The capability of the poet to step out of her culture and lan-
guage evidently endows her with a divine perspective that is both
cruelly objective and immensely compassionate. From that alien
distance she looks at things and humans as they interact, and can
depict them as toys. Such an absurdity of human actions in war
seems to saturate Mikhail's poetry with two overlapping layers of
emotions: sadness and incredulity. Sadness because the world for
the child speaker is not fun; incredulity because the only safe play-
ground left for the child in a war zone is to mentally transform
insensitive humans into toys. It is revealing that Mikhail, in one of
her statements on poetry, views poetry as play, a complex game like
chess, with all the characters being fated by the designated rules of
engagement and the imagination of the players. Significantly, one
of the poems in the collection is titled "Game," which depicts a
game of chess wherein the speaker pities not only pawns, but also
the players, who are ultimately controlled by irrational gods:

He is a poor player
moved by an empty life
without black or white.
It is a poor life
moved by a bewildered god
who once tried to play with clay.

If the creator of the universe is "bewildered," human rationality, reasoning, civilization, religion, history all become as gratuitous as the mosquito's life in Nietzsche's "On Truth and Lies."

Frequently in world literature when immense absurdity collides with human consciousness, the usual human reaction is a mixture of sardonic laughter and sorrow, not unlike black humor in American literature. In Mikhail's delicate, highly sensitive poetry there is a jarring streak of blackness. This blend of harshness and sensitivity is simultaneously pleasing and unsettling, aggravating our sense of the familiar:

> I thank everyone I don't love.
> They don't cause me heartache;
> they don't make me write long letters;
> they don't disturb my dreams.
> I don't await them anxiously;
> I don't read their horoscopes in magazines;
> I don't dial their numbers;
> I don't think of them.
> I thank them a lot.
> They don't turn my life upside down.

By employing fresh idioms and phrases to express her unusual, defamiliarizing view of the world, Mikhail liberates our thoughts and feelings from the stringency of fossilized everyday language. And I am equally moved by her poetry in Arabic and in Elizabeth Winslow's intuitive and elegant translations that facilitate the full passage of this poetry into English without significant loss of its Iraqi-Arabic symbolic order.

Early in 1999, the poet Naomi Shihab Nye introduced me to Elizabeth Winslow as a good translator from the Arabic. She consulted with me on her translations of Palestinian poet Mahmoud Shuqair. I was so impressed with her perceptive understanding of the language and the culture of the Arabs that I invited her to contribute to *Iraqi Poetry Today*, encouraging her to translate some poems by Mikhail. It was a thrilling experience. Winslow was deeply moved by Mikhail's poetry, which became a kind of muse for her translations. From her I learned that proficiency in two languages is not enough to produce the best translations; the translator must not only fall in love with the text, but also have the irresistible urge to possess the text by rewriting it into her native language. The translated work, even if it is done by the same author, is a product of two creative minds.

As a teacher of English literature, I think Mikhail's poetry, in its wittiness and ingenuity, its playfulness and stimulating vision of the world, might remind many readers of the poetry of Emily Dickinson, and some of the metaphysical qualities of John Donne's poetry, particularly the adroit conceits from the sciences. Her "Theory of Absence," in which a geometrical theorem becomes a metaphor for love, resembles in its inventiveness, Donne's powerful use of the compass as an extended metaphor in "A Valediction Forbidding Mourning." Mikhail's lexical austerity, on the one hand, is reminiscent of Dickinson's suggestive elliptical poetics, and on the other hand recalls the traditional Sufi dictum: "The wider the vision, the smaller the sentence becomes."

—Saadi Simawe

THE WAR
WORKS HARD

الحرب تعمل بجد

ONE
THE WAR WORKS HARD

(2004)

Bag of Bones

What good luck!
She has found his bones.
The skull is also in the bag
the bag in her hand
like all other bags
in all other trembling hands.
His bones, like thousands of bones
in the mass graveyard,
his skull, not like any other skull.
Two eyes or holes
with which he saw too much,
two ears
with which he listened to music
that told his own story,
a nose
that never knew clean air,
a mouth, open like a chasm,
was not like that when he kissed her
there, quietly,
not in this place
noisy with skulls and bones and dust
dug up with questions:
What does it mean to die all this death
in a place where the darkness plays all this silence?
What does it mean to meet your loved ones now
with all of these hollow places?
To give back to your mother
on the occasion of death

a handful of bones
she had given to you
on the occasion of birth?
To depart without death or birth certificates
because the dictator does not give receipts
when he takes your life?
The dictator has a heart, too,
a balloon that never pops.
He has a skull, too, a huge one
not like any other skull.
It solved by itself a math problem
that multiplied the one death by millions
to equal homeland.
The dictator is the director of a great tragedy.
He has an audience, too,
an audience that claps
until the bones begin to rattle—
the bones in the bags,
the full bag finally in her hand,
unlike her disappointed neighbor
who has not yet found her own.

Shoemaker

A skillful shoemaker
throughout his life
has pounded the nails
and smoothed the leather
for a variety of feet:
feet that flee
feet that kick
feet that plunge
feet that pursue
feet that run
feet that trample
feet that collapse
feet that jump
feet that trip
feet that are still
feet that tremble
feet that dance
feet that return . . .
Life is a handful of nails
in the hand of a shoemaker.

The War Works Hard

How magnificent the war is!
How eager
and efficient!
Early in the morning,
it wakes up the sirens
and dispatches ambulances
to various places,
swings corpses through the air,
rolls stretchers to the wounded,
summons rain
from the eyes of mothers,
digs into the earth
dislodging many things
from under the ruins . . .
Some are lifeless and glistening,
others are pale and still throbbing . . .
It produces the most questions
in the minds of children,
entertains the gods
by shooting fireworks and missiles
into the sky,
sows mines in the fields
and reaps punctures and blisters,
urges families to emigrate,
stands beside the clergymen
as they curse the devil
(poor devil, he remains
with one hand in the searing fire) . . .
The war continues working, day and night.
It inspires tyrants

to deliver long speeches,
awards medals to generals
and themes to poets.
It contributes to the industry
of artificial limbs,
provides food for flies,
adds pages to the history books,
achieves equality
between killer and killed,
teaches lovers to write letters,
accustoms young women to waiting,
fills the newspapers
with articles and pictures,
builds new houses
for the orphans,
invigorates the coffin makers,
gives grave diggers
a pat on the back
and paints a smile on the leader's face.
The war works with unparalleled diligence!
Yet no one gives it
a word of praise.

The Game

He is a poor pawn.
He always jumps to the next square.
He doesn't turn left or right
and doesn't look back.
He is moved by a foolish queen
who cuts across the board
lengthwise and diagonally.
She doesn't tire of carrying the medals
and cursing the bishops.
She is a poor queen
moved by a reckless king
who counts the squares every day
and claims that they are diminishing.
He arranges the knights and rooks
and dreams of a stubborn opponent.
He is a poor king
moved by an experienced player
who rubs his head
and loses his time in an endless game.
He is a poor player
moved by an empty life
without black or white.
It is a poor life
moved by a bewildered god
who once tried to play with clay.
He is a poor god.
He doesn't know how
to escape
from his dilemma.

The Prisoner

She doesn't understand
what it means to be "guilty."
She waits at the prison entrance
until she sees him, to say,
"Take care of yourself,"
as she always used to remind him
when he went off to school,
when he left for work,
when he returned while on vacation.
She doesn't understand
what they are saying now
at the back of the podium
in their official uniforms.
They report that he should be kept there
with lonely strangers.
It never occurred to her,
as she sang lullabies on his bed
in those distant days,
someday, he would end up in this cold place
without windows or moons.
She doesn't understand,
the prisoner's mother doesn't understand
why she should leave him
just because
"the visit is over."

A Drop of Water

for Mazin

The snowboy was thinking of the snowgirl
when desire burned his heart,
the fire spreading
until he gradually melted
and disappeared . . .
The snowgirl is frozen in a drop of a water.
Perhaps this is a token of the snowboy?
She thinks this and melts,
shrinking as she thinks
and the drop grows.

Inanna

I am Inanna.
And this is my city.
And this is our meeting
round, red and full.
Here, sometime ago,
someone was asking for help
shortly before his death.
Houses were still here
with their roofs,
people,
and noise.
Palm trees
were about to whisper something to me
before they were beheaded
like some foreigners in my country.
I see my old neighbors
on the TV
running
from bombs,
sirens
and Abu Al-Tubar.
I see my new neighbors
on the sidewalks
running
for their morning exercises.
I am here
thinking of the relationship
between the mouse and the computer.
I search you on the Internet.
I distinguish you

grave by grave,
skull by skull,
bone by bone.
I see you
in my dreams.
I see the antiquities
scattered
and broken
in the museum.
My necklaces are among them.
I yell at you:
Behave, you sons of the dead!
Stop fighting
over my clothes and gold!
How you disturb my sleep
and frighten a flock of kisses
out of my nation!
You planted pomegranates and prisons
round, red and full.
These are your holes in my robe.
And this is our meeting . . .

An Urgent Call

This is an urgent call
for the American soldier Lynndie
to immediately return to her homeland.
She suffers from a dangerous virus
in her heart.
She is pregnant
and is sinking in deep mud.
She sinks deeper and deeper
as she hears: "Good job!"
Hurry up, Lynndie,
go back to America now.
Don't worry,
you will not lose your job.
There are prisons everywhere,
prisons with big black holes,
and great shivering,
and consecutive flashes,
and tremblings that convey messages
with no language
in a blind galaxy.
Don't worry,
nobody will force you
to feed the birds
when you carry a gun.
Nobody will force you
to work for the environment
when you wear combat boots.
Don't worry,
we will send an email to God
to tell Him

that the barbarians
were the solution.
Don't worry.
Take a sick leave
and release your baby
from your body,
but don't forget
to hide those terrible pictures,
the pictures of you dancing in the mud.
Keep them away
from his or her eyes.
Hide them, please.
You don't want your child to cry out:
The prisoners are naked . . .

Non-Military Statements

1
Yes, I did write in my letter
that I would wait for you forever.
I didn't mean exactly "forever,"
I just included it for the rhythm.

 2
No, he was not among them.
There were so many of them!
More than I've seen in my life
on any television screen.
And yet he was not among them.

3
It has no carvings
or arms.
It always remains there
in front of the television
this empty chair.

4
I dream of a magic wand
that changes my kisses to stars.
At night you can gaze at them
and know they are innumerable.

5
I thank everyone I don't love.
They don't cause me heartache;
they don't make me write long letters;

they don't disturb my dreams.
I don't wait for them anxiously;
I don't read their horoscopes in magazines;
I don't dial their numbers;
I don't think of them.
I thank them a lot.
They don't turn my life upside down.

6
I drew a door
to sit behind, ready
to open the door
as soon as you arrive.

Between Two Wars

This is all that remains:
a handful of burnt papers,
photos, here and there
with rippled backs like maps.
One of us died,
another savors life
in his place.
One of us returned,
changed by magic into a small bird
who knows the news in another language.
One of us went crazy
and kept babbling nonsense
for hours under the sun.
One of us escaped
from the bugs and the officers
to who knows where.
Sidewalk vendors wrap falafel
in the pages of our books.
The entire assembly of gods
has come to help.
On the way to us, they pinch their noses
and watch a woman roll tobacco.
To her, the hand-rolled cigarette
is more wondrous
than the Seven Wonders of the World.
All her relatives have gone abroad.
The boy next door
returned one day,
a tin star on his chest.
He talked too much

about that star
until, one day, he changed
into a piece of metal
in the Martyrs' Monument.
This is all that remains:
a handful of meaningless words
engraved on the walls.
We read so absent-mindedly,
eventually we forget
how, in the short lull
between two wars,
we became so old.

Tough Rose

I am a new rose.
My redness, wild hallucinations,
and my thorns, prison cells
with views of the moon.
Yesterday someone touched me,
but did not pick me.
I was tough.
I didn't give him any of my petals.
Tomorrow when people pass by,
my leaves will remind them
of things that never were,
and they will leave my dry head bare
contemplating the new roses
which were not here yesterday.

The Jewel

It no longer stretches across the river.
It is not in the city,
not on the map.
The bridge that was . . .
The bridge that we were . . .
The Pontoon Bridge
we crossed every day . . .
Dropped by the war into the river
just like the blue jewel
that lady dropped
off the side of the Titanic.

A Voice

I want to return
return
return
return
repeated the parrot
in the room where
her owner had left her
alone
to repeat:
return
return
return . . .

Travel Agency

A pile of travelers is on the table.
Tomorrow their planes will take off
and dot the sky with silver
and descend like evening on the cities.
Mr. George says that his beloved
no longer smiles at him.
He wants to travel directly to Rome
to dig a grave there like her smile.
"But not all roads lead to Rome," I remind him,
and hand him a ticket for one.
He wants to sit by the window
to be sure that the sky
is the same
everywhere.

0

a heart bleeds   bewildering siren   imperfect pulses

red light   red light   imperfect pulses   imperfect pulses   bewildering siren

tears flow   a heart bleeds   bewildering siren   they drive the stretcher

they bring flowers   a heart bleeds   they bring flowers   they bring flowers   they drive the stretcher   tears flow

rushing ambulance   a heart bleeds   to the grave   imperfect pulses   bewildering siren   they bring flowers   they drive the stretcher

they bring flowers   red light   they bring flowers   rushing ambulance   bewildering siren   they carry the coffin

tears flow   red light   to the emergency room   tears flow   a heart bleeds   rushing ambulance

red light   imperfect pulses   a heart bleeds   they carry the coffin   rushing ambulance   they carry the coffin

to the emergency room   to the coffin   rushing ambulance   to the emergency room

to the grave

23

Santa Claus

With his beard long like war
and his suit red like history,
Santa Claus paused with a smile
and asked me to pick something.
You're a good girl, he said,
therefore you deserve a toy.
Then he gave me something like poetry,
and because I hesitated,
he assured me: Don't be afraid, little one,
I am Santa Claus.
I distribute beautiful toys to children.
Haven't you seen me before?
I replied: But the Santa Claus I know
wears a military uniform,
and each year he distributes
red swords,
dolls for orphans,
artificial limbs,
and photos of the missing
to be hung on the walls.

Buzz

As the airplane takes off
and puffs out a smoke of images,
I think about tossing one of my ears
from the window.
It has an annoying buzz that abrades me.
The buzz smells like gunpowder
and trips the pretty words
which bubble out accidentally
from my other ear
to the friendly sky
vanishing in clouds.
The stewardess doesn't know
why I block my ear with my hand
and puff out images of smoke.
I don't know why
the memories grow
while I shrink.
I don't remember what I wanted to say.
I don't want to say
what I remember
as the plane lands.

Crashed Acts

After an hour delay,
the plane took off with its busy passengers . . .
The stewardess will not smile.
The student will not read his letter.
The actress will not play the role of princess.
The business man will not attend the meeting.
The husband will not see his wife.
The teacher will not wear her glasses.
The university graduate will not start her new job.
The lover will not celebrate his beloved's birthday.
The lawyer will not defend the client.
The retiree will not be there.
The child will not ask
any more questions.

Snowstorm

for Lori

Oh, what sweet children!
They rush to awaken us.
We, the snow-women,
just now born
from nostalgia or boredom,
accumulate outside
making the pampered storm
wade through our flakes.
Sometimes the storm covers us
like an earnest god
with leaves from the trees of Paradise.
And we, the snow-women,
kneaded in the children's sweet hands,
expand and smile,
and when they attach our eyes,
we gaze gratefully,
staring to make them hurry.
We can't wait for them to attach our feet.
We want to move,
the celebration will start soon.
We will signal with our fingers
which they are now forming.
We will signal
to a balloon
that rises from our voices.
There it is!
Look!
We can't wait
to get moving.
They are taking too long

to attach our feet
so that we—
how sad!
—depart on a sunny day.

To Any Other Place

With her unkempt hair
and her repugnant smell
and her fleeing children,
The Red Mother sat
face to face
with The Brown Mother
and a third, The Wordless Conversation:
The Red Mother said: How much I hate you!
Your beginning is my end.
The Brown Mother said: Your sons, the battles,
shatter the glass of our windows
and terrify my sleeping daughters.
The Red Mother: I want firewood . . . firewood . . .
I want to feed my sons,
I want them to grow up
and devour your daughters, the peace.
The Brown Mother: I raise my daughters for roses
and you raise your sons for ashes.
The fire breaks out
and the dancing will start around it.
The fire is not satisfied
and the dance does not end.
The Red Mother: Let us celebrate every year
the steps which have diminished
and the pairs of shoes that remained
there in the mud.
The Brown Mother: This rhythm
does not please me,
and these drums make the din
of emptiness.

I want to move my daughters
to another place,
to any other place . . .

I Was In A Hurry

Yesterday I lost a country.
I was in a hurry,
and didn't notice when it fell from me
like a broken branch from a forgetful tree.
Please, if anyone passes by
and stumbles across it,
perhaps in a suitcase
open to the sky,
or engraved on a rock
like a gaping wound,
or wrapped
in the blankets of emigrants,
or canceled
like a losing lottery ticket,
or helplessly forgotten
in Purgatory,
or rushing forward without a goal
like the questions of children,
or rising with the smoke of war,
or rolling in a helmet on the sand,
or stolen in Ali Baba's jar,
or disguised in the uniform of a policeman
who stirred up the prisoners
and fled,
or squatting in the mind of a woman
who tries to smile,
or scattered
like the dreams
of new immigrants in America.
If anyone stumbles across it,

return it to me, please.
Please return it, sir.
Please return it, madam.
It is my country . . .
I was in a hurry
when I lost it yesterday.

America

Please don't ask me, America.
I don't remember
on which street,
with whom,
or under which star.
Don't ask me . . .
I don't remember
the colors of the people
or their signatures.
I don't remember if they had
our faces
and our dreams,
if they were singing
or not,
writing from the left
or the right
or not writing at all,
sleeping in houses
on sidewalks
or in airports,
making love or not making love.
Please don't ask me, America.
I don't remember their names
or their birthplaces.
People are grass—
they grow everywhere, America.
Don't ask me . . .
I don't remember
what time it was,
what the weather was like,

which language,
or which flag.
Don't ask me . . .
I don't remember
how long they walked under the sun
or how many died.
I don't remember
the shapes of the boats
or the number of stops . . .
How many suitcases they carried
or left behind,
if they came complaining
or without complaint.
Stop your questioning, America,
and offer your hand
to the tired
on the other shore.
Offer it without questions
or waiting lists.
What good is it to gain the whole world
if you lose your soul, America?
Who said that the sky
would lose all of its stars
if night passed without answers?
America, leave your questionnaires to the river
and leave me to my lover.
It has been a long time,
we are two distant, rippling shores
and the river wriggles between us
like a well-cooked fish.
It has been a long time, America,
(longer than the stories of my grandmother
in the evening)

and we are waiting for the signal
to throw our shell in the river.
We know that the river is full
of shells
this last one
wouldn't matter,
yet it matters to the shell . . .
Why do you ask all these questions?
You want our fingerprints
in all languages
and I have become old,
older than my father.
He used to tell me in the evenings
when no trains ran:
One day, we will go to America.
One day, we will go
and sing a song,
translated or not translated,
at the Statue of Liberty.
And now, America, now
I come to you without my father.
The dead ripen faster
than Indian figs,
but they never grow older, America.
They come in shifts of shadow and light
in our dreams
and as shooting stars
or curve in rainbows
over the houses we left behind.
They sometimes get angry
if we keep them waiting long . . .
What time is it now?
I am afraid I will receive

your registered mail, America,
in this hour
which is good for nothing . . .
So I will toy with the freedom
like teasing a pet cat.
I wouldn't know what else
to do with it
in this hour
which is good for nothing . . .
And my sweetheart
there, on the opposite
shore of the river
carries a flower for me.
And I—as you know—
dislike faded flowers.
I do like my sweetheart's handwriting
shining each day in the mail.
I salvage it from among ad fliers
and a special offer:
"Buy One Get One Free"
and an urgent promotional announcement:
"Win a million dollars
if you subscribe to this magazine!"
and bills to be paid
in monthly installments.
I like my sweetheart's handwriting,
though it gets shakier every day.
We have a single picture
just one picture, America.
I want it.
I want that moment
(forever out of reach)
in the picture which I know

from every angle:
the circular moment of sky.
Imagine, America,
if one of us drops out of the picture
and leaves the album full
of loneliness,
or if life becomes
a camera
without film.
Imagine, America!
Without a frame,
the night will take us
tomorrow,
darling,
tomorrow
the night
will take us
without a frame.
We will shake the museums
forever from their sleep,
fix our broken clocks
so we'll tick in the public squares
whenever the train
passes us by.
Tomorrow,
darling,
tomorrow
we will bloom:
two leaves of a tree
we will try not to be
too graceful and green
and in time
we will tumble down like dancers

taken by the wind
to the places whose names
we'll have forgotten.
We will be glad for the sake of turtles
because they persist along their way . . .
Tomorrow
darling,
tomorrow,
I'll look at your eyes
to see your new wrinkles,
the lines of our future dreams.
As you braid my gray hair
under rain
or sun
or moon,
every hair will know
that nothing happens
twice,
every kiss a country
with a history
a geography
and a language
with joy and sadness
with war
and ruins
and holidays
and ticking clocks . . .
And when the pain in your neck returns, darling,
you will not have time to complain
and won't be concerned.
The pain will remain inside us
coy as snow that won't melt.
Tomorrow, darling,

tomorrow,
two rings will jingle
in the wooden box.
They have been shining for a long time
on two trembling hands,
entangled
by the absence.
Tomorrow,
the whiteness will expose
all its colors
as we celebrate the return
of what was lost
or concealed
in the whiteness.
How should I know, America,
which of the colors
was the most joyful
tumultuous
alienated
or assimilated
of them all?
How would I know, America?

Silent Movie

There,
in the sky's playground,
the gods toss us around like curses
and cast us down from above
without speaking a word.
They watch us,
but don't hear us.
We are a silent movie
with a bad director.
No wonder the gods get bored
or switch us off and go to sleep
or forget about us
as we bend like a question mark
on an empty screen
or sneeze as we pray
for the return of the gods
even without any words.

Laheeb and the City

Yes, I love those children, who ran laughing after me. They didn't believe a thing I said. (I am not a prophet to be denied). They hid in their mother's dresses and left my dead dog without food, so he does not wag his tail for them. He has not wagged his tail for a long time. And yet I've been here for quite some time, and this is my city which no longer wags its tail, and those are the children whom I love but from a distance. I don't like to see them for more than a few minutes because, after that, they run after me shouting. I don't know who told whom that what happened did not happen in this or any other place. It refers without watch-hands or numbers to that event which has not happened in this or any other city, neither more, nor less.

The Rocking Chair

When they came,
the aunt was still there
on the rocking chair.
For thirty years
she rocked . . .
Now
that death has asked for her hand,
she has departed
without a word,
leaving the chair
alone
rocking.

Traces

I wonder if you will guess
how many tremors passed between these walls?
Can you distinguish
between the tremors of fear
from the bombing
and the tremors of kisses?
Between a corner that hid us from the sounds,
and another, where we hid under the photographs?
I wonder if these windows will reflect for you
a few of our waitings,
our comings and goings
between the door and the wall,
our grasping at any rumors or news?
I wonder if you will guess
how many songs were raucously sung
in the topmost room
where wakefulness still remains?
I wonder if you will guess,
when you stumble on this high threshold,
what footsteps have passed here?
Do you know who returned
and who did not return?
I wonder if you will guess
you, who will live in our house,
I wonder if you will guess,
how sometimes
nothing matters.

The Foreigner

1
On a foreign tree
in a foreign field
he threw me a fleeting glance
like a fragment of sky
between skyscrapers.
He is a foreign bird
who abandoned the foreign nest
on the foreign tree
in the foreign field
and left behind, me, the foreigner,
contemplating the tremble of the branch
after the foreign bird
has flown.

2
I don't know a thing
about my role in this new play
and all my lines
will mean nothing to the audience
since they understand
neither my Aramaic
nor my Arabic.
So I'll imitate the gestures
of whomever I encounter
on the road
as I guess
their facial expressions
under the foreign sky.
I won't tremble
more than a baby

leaving the test tube
against his will.
And I won't cry
despite all these bodies
who greet me
kindly and carelessly.
I have already seen them in a dream.
Like me, they rush to prove
they exist.
They have fingerprints
and memories
and wings
and like me, they sometimes
get stricken with boredom
and the flu.
They too depart
for new places,
though as tourists
and not immigrants.
It is not enough, after all,
to complain of the climate
or of my role
in this new play.

Five Minutes

In five minutes, the world will end . . .
The owner of the shop next door
has just put up the "Closed" sign
and gone away
as if he knows there is no time left for work.
There are other stores open.
Their owners are still absorbed in work,
but the world will end in . . .
A group of lively boys
rushes by in the street;
following them, a dog
leading an old man.
The traffic light is red.
The bus driver makes a slight adjustment
to the rearview mirror.
There are still several scenes
that move across the mirror.
The driver pulls away now.
The traffic light is green.
It will keep changing, even after
five minutes!
A young man checks his watch
and waits for the next bus . . .
In the public park, a couple walks past the statues
and smiles under the sun.
The statues are carefree.
They stare firmly at nothing.
A tourist wanders full of curiosity
and takes pictures of what will soon be absent.
There, in the white hospital,

women bear new babies
too late.
The babies might leave the world
without names.
In one of the wards,
they will be left
forever in test tubes
while the wiggling lab mouse
performing a test
will be free at last
from the big eye that always watches.
The test is not difficult,
but time will run out
before the answer.
And it no longer matters
whether or not you knew.
Smell the roses and keep going.
The rose always knows
that the world will end in five minutes . . .
The blue shirt in the shop window
seems beautiful on the mannequin.
A young woman points it out to her friend
and they head toward the revolving door
to be swallowed by the towering building . . .
On the wall, glossy advertisements:
HUGE SALE!
NEW REMEDY FOR WRINKLES!
CIGARETTES DON'T HARM YOUR HEALTH!
but the world will end . . .
In his walled room
inside the walled palace
inside the walled city,
the tyrant is chewing on an apple

and watching himself on television.
Who would believe that in five minutes
he will relinquish his throne?
Another defendant receives a life sentence.
His attorney wants an appeal
but the world will . . .
Passengers push through the exit door
others come in through the entrance door.
A woman sets down her suitcase
and waves her hand
(it is not me).
A man waves to her from behind the airport glass
(it is not you).
I don't know if they met
or if the time . . .
That university student
prefers to travel by train.
It doesn't make much difference now.
He has agreed with a friend
to go on a picnic.
I don't know if the picnic ended before the world
or the world before the picnic!
As for me, I am writing a letter.
I don't think it will be finished
within five minutes.

TWO
FROM ALMOST MUSIC
(1997)

The Cup

The woman turned the cup upside down
among the letters.
She extinguished the lights except one candle
and placed her finger on the cup
and repeated words like an incantation:
O spirit . . . If you are present, answer Yes.
And then the cup moved to the right for YES.
The woman said: Are you truly my husband, the martyr?
The cup moved to the right for YES.
She said: Why did you leave me so soon?
The cup moved to the letters—
IT WAS NOT IN MY HANDS.
She said: Why didn't you escape?
The cup moved to the letters—
I ESCAPED.
She said: Then how were you killed?
The cup moved—FROM BEHIND.
She said: And what will I do now
with all this loneliness?
The cup did not move.
She said: Do you love me?
The cup moved to the right for YES.
She said: Can I make you stay here?
The cup moved to the left for NO.
She said: Can I come with you?
The cup moved to the left.
She said: Will our lives change?
The cup moved to the right.
She said: When?
The cup moved—1996.

She said: Are you at peace?
The cup moved reluctantly to YES.
She said: What should I do?
The cup moved—ESCAPE.
She said: To where?
The cup did not move.
She said: Will we experience more misfortune?
The cup did not move.
She said: What do you want me to do?
The cup moved to a meaningless sentence.
She said: Are you tired of my questions?
The cup moved to the left.
She said: Can I ask more?
The cup did not move.
After a silence, she mumbled:
O spirit . . . Go in peace.
She turned the cup over
and blew out the candle
and called to her son
who was in the garden catching insects
with a helmet full of holes.

The Resonance

The resonance inside me
finally fell into the water.
On the shore of the world I sit looking at it,
and you watch me from the other shore.
You watch the sound as it fades away.
You watch the ripples as they disappear.
You watch the stars swing down.
You watch silver gleam on the scales of fish.
You watch something that breaks under the sun.
You watch as I dive into the sound,
and then you reach out

ح ب ا ل/ص و ت ك / أ ل ش م س ي /ف ن ا ل ه ا/ أ ل
ر ن ي ن

Hibal sutek il-shamsy fanalaha-il-raneen:
Ropes of your sun-filled sound are reined by the resonance.
The letters spread in the water like this:

ح ب / ا ل ص و ت / ك ا ل ش م س / ي ف ن ا /ل ه ـ / أ
ل ر ن ي ن

Hub il-sut kal-shamsi yafna lahu il-raneen:
Love of the sound is like the sun
for which the resonance will perish.

The Artist Child

—I want to draw the sky.
—Draw it, my darling.
—I have.
—And why do you spread
the colors this way?
—Because the sky
has no edges.

. . .

—I want to draw the earth.
—Draw it, my darling.
—I have.
—And who is this?
—She is my friend.
—And where is the earth?
—In her handbag.

. . .

—I want to draw the moon.
—Draw it, my darling.
—I can't.
—Why?
—The waves shatter it
continuously.

. . .

—I want to draw paradise.
—Draw it, my darling.
—I have.
—But I don't see any colors.
—It is colorless.

. . .

—I want to draw the war.
—Draw it, my darling.
—I have.
—And what is this circle?
—Guess.
—A drop of blood?
—No.
—A bullet?
—No.
—Then, what?
—The button
that turns off the lights.

The Departure of Friends

The country left my jar.
My friends left the country.
Everything perished, except the country's dust.
I took a handful,
and formed a statue from the darkness.
I held up a candelabra to the statue.
Whose tear is this?
What is this that melts?
Why do things return to dust?
I took a handful,
and formed another jar.
I urged the jar to leave the country.
Why is the jar empty inside?
Whose absence drops
and makes the rain fall like the gods?
I want something new under the sun.
I beat the rain with my stick.
Dust from a broken jar
flows into my hand.

A Tombstone

Blessed is the fruit of my heart (my loss),
curved with tenderness
like an inverted hollow.
Here I am
coldly counting all the flowers
thrown on my corpse.
They are busy pounding in the nails
while, by mistake, my dreams still leap
inside the coffin,
confused by the excess
of sparrows in my slumber
(without wings they plunged into my sleep).
—Who dreams, in my place?—
You who fill my skull with ashes, please
destroy my memories completely
(the bells ring endlessly).
The gravedigger is preoccupied . . .
And I, without concern, wipe away
the dust from my immortality
and gaze toward:

هنا ترقد على رجاء القيامة
مواطنة صالحة للنسيان.

Here in the hope of resurrection lies
a suitable citizen for oblivion.

The Theory of Absence

The hypothesis: I am tense and so are you.
We neither meet nor separate.

The desired result: We meet in the absence.

The proof: As tension turns people into arcs, we are two arcs.
We neither meet nor separate (the hypothesis)
so we must be parallel.
If two parallel lines are bisected by a third line
(in this case, the line of tension)
their corresponding angles must be equal (a geometrical theorem).
So we are congruent (because shapes are congruent
when their angles are equal)
and we form a circle (since the sum
of two congruent arcs
is a circle).
Therefore, we meet in the absence
(since the circumference of a circle
is the sum of contiguous points
which can each be considered
a point of contact).

Nothing Here is Enough

I need a parrot,
identical days,
a quantity of needles,
and artificial ink
to make history.

I need veiled eyelids,
black lines,
and ruined puppets
to make geography.

I need a sky wider than longing,
and water that is not H_2O
to make wings.

The days are no longer enough
to distinguish the missing.
I no longer see you
because I no longer dream.
I offer a tear to the rain
as if scattering you
in the Dead Sea,
and in order to sing you,
I need glass to muffle the sound.

What's New?

I saw a ghost pass in the mirror.
Someone whispered something in my ear.
I said a word, and left.
Graves were scattered with mandrake seeds.
A bleating sound entered the assembly.
Gardens remained hanging.
Straw was scattered with the words.
No fruit is left.
Someone climbed on the shoulders of another.
Someone descended into the netherworld.
Other things are happening
in secret.
I don't know what they are—
this is everything.

The Pomegranate Seeds

A long time has passed since we were first imprisoned
in the pomegranate.
In vain we rush and strike the interior surface with our heads,
hoping that a hole might open for us,
so that we could meet the air just once . . .
Our losses increase each day.
Some of the seeds sacrificed their juice for freedom
as they ripped their way through the trenches.
I told my sisters, the pomegranate seeds:
The dents which begin to appear on the surface
prove the existence of a fist
which threatens our destiny and squeezes our hopes.
What are your suggestions for our liberation?
—Shall we stay close together?
—We will be smothered by the strain of togetherness.
—Shall we ask a higher power for help?
—No one will hear our shouts through this enveloping shell.
—Shall we wait for a savior?
—We will rot before anyone thinks of us.
—Then we should stand in circles, like impossible holes.
Before the circles were completed, a hole began to open by itself.
We wanted to dance a dabka,
but a worm reared its head over the terrified seeds.
The pomegranate began to shake,
a great crack appeared on the surface.
Some of the seeds trembled inside the human fist,
others were stripped off onto the ground . . .
I am still suspended in the cavity
and the worm lies in ambush for me . . .

With One Look From Him

He broke the frame . . .
With one look, he broke it.
The yellow emerged bearing disease.
The blue emerged with one foot in the sea
and one in the sky.
The red emerged as wars.
The white emerged with braids.
The black emerged as the disgrace of his friend.
The green emerged looking back.
The inside became the outside.
I emerged inside the empty canvas.
With one look from him
I emerged.

An Orange

From another star
I roll endlessly
and sink deeper in the river
of no return.
With invisible nets
I catch whatever numbers I find
and scatter them all to zero.
I sit on top of death
like a pile of smoke
and cry
because the orange peeled
from our laughter
is not the globe of the earth.

THREE
FROM THE PSALMS OF ABSENCE
(1993)

Behind the Glass

Today . . .
everything hangs on a bulletin board.
The scene ages in ruins
and the audience, divided by war,
reunites in the absence.
The curtain falls
on the day's last shiver.
The moon is an aspirin tablet.
The villages are perforated like memory,
the sky a cap for airplanes
with no room for birds.
I flow wing-like behind a glass
that exchanges endless brokenness with me
for a universe of darkness
that splinters into the non-horizon.
I watch the dead rise from the glass
like rainbows.
Shall we give the air
another lung
or remain behind the glass
from one demise to another?

I borrow false feet
from the amoebae
and depart.
I dream of the vanishing point
and weightlessness,
but dream is an out-dated word
like my sadness in the presence
of the universe's last day.

Today,
everything hangs on a bulletin board.

The Nun

The mountains are changeable,
the nun left the convent:
She doesn't understand geography.

The church bells are dead,
the nun took the shape of a circle:
She rings.

The prayers are repeated,
the nun broke up into her original stones:
She recites the Act of Forgetfulness.

Eternity is at a loss,
the nun sways between the sea and the sky:
She thinks of another blueness.

The New Year

1
There is a knock at the door.
How disappointing . . .
It is the New Year and not you.

2
I don't know how to add your absence to my life.
I don't know how to subtract myself from it.
I don't know how to divide it
among the laboratory flasks.

3
Time stopped at twelve o'clock
and confused the watchmaker.
There were no flaws with the watch.
It was just a matter of the hands
which embraced and forgot the world.

Transformations of the Child and the Moon

FIRST IMAGE

The child raised his head to see
the moon concealed
behind the building.
Their shadows chased each other.
The building didn't know
who jumped first
to paint a red puddle
under the child's feet.

SECOND IMAGE

The child went to the river,
and as a likeness to a mirror,
the child sank
into the river's drowning moon.

THIRD IMAGE

The child raced on the beach
chasing the falling ball of the sky,
while the sand counted
the footprints of the moon
carrying the child to heaven.

The Chaldean's Ruins

Ascetic,
he emerges from her belly to the grave.
His days are not entered on the calendar,
and he does not gather the things that are scattered.
Earthquakes do not move him nor wink at death without him.
Was he born before the earth
or after her wails?
A wind blew by
and did not shake the tree.
They said: It was no wind,
but his sighing.
He is the unsettled Chaldean
and it was no tree,
but the elongated roots of his village.
Dried out,
he releases water into the fields
then brays on the hill.
During the day he is content with darkness.
Homeless,
exile squeezes him
and discards his rind
to the skyscrapers.
Waiting,
he lights a candle before the Virgin.
Perhaps she will shift the borders toward him.
Hallelujah . . . Hallelujah . . .
He celebrates the coming of his sheep
and holds a vigil at their graves
until morning comes.
Bewildered,

he turns the mountains between his hands
searching for a speck of homeland.
Far from his tent,
he tightens the ropes
and accumulates like sand
in distant countries.
Preserved
in a can, he writes on his forehead:
MADE IN RUINS
and feels that the word "ruins"
is enough to refer to
what has happened
or what remains.

The Shadow of a Tear

In a time of quick greetings
and artificial lights,
the shadow of a tear
falls across the sky.
Neither the rushing wheels
nor the road
nor the eraser
can stop it.

Above the branches
fly careless birds.
One lags behind the flock,
but don't worry.
He will catch up in a little while;
he is only distracted
by the shadow of a tear
broken on the branches.

Pronouns

He plays a train.
She plays a whistle.
They move away.

He plays a rope.
She plays a tree.
They swing.

He plays a dream.
She plays a feather.
They fly.

He plays a general.
She plays people.
They declare war.

NOTES

PAGE

11 *Inanna*: Sumerian goddess of love, fertility, procreation, and war; the first goddess of recorded history.

   Abu Al-Tubar: "The hatchet man," a serial killer in Baghdad during the 1970s who was later discovered to be an evil hand of the Baathist regime.

13 *Lynndie*: Lynndie England, one of the seven U.S. army reservists prosecuted in the Abu Ghraib prison scandal. Photographs showed her and other U.S. soldiers torturing Iraqi detainees. Whether or not they acted under orders of the Pentagon and the White House is still under investigation.

18 *Martyrs' Monument*: The Monument of Saddam's Qadissiya Martyrs, designed by the sculptor Ismaayl Fatah Al-Turk, commemorates the Iraqi soldiers who died during the Iran-Iraq War. After the U.S. occupation of Iraq, its site was turned into an American military base.

34 *and the river wriggles between us / like a well-cooked fish*: A reference to how restaurants along the Tigris cook fish by constantly turning it over a wood fire.

41 *Laheeb*: Laheeb Numan, a trial lawyer in Baghdad who was imprisoned and tortured for standing up in court against Saddam Hussein's son Uday. Nevertheless, after the U.S.-led overthrow of Hussein's government, she organized a children's protest against the occupation.

51 *The cup moved—1996*: About "The Cup," Mikhail says: "This poem was written and published in 1994. By chance, in 1996, I arrived in America. I didn't know the significance of 1996 when I wrote the poem, but later realized it came true for me. I mean that my life was changed forever in 1996."

61 *dabka*: A popular traditional folk dance of the Arabic-speaking world.